CAMBRIDGE
UNIVERSITY PRESS

Cambridge Lower Secondary
Science

ENGLISH LANGUAGE SKILLS WORKBOOK 7

Mary Jones & Sally Burbeary

CAMBRIDGE
UNIVERSITY PRESS

University Printing House, Cambridge CB2 8BS, United Kingdom

One Liberty Plaza, 20th Floor, New York, NY 10006, USA

477 Williamstown Road, Port Melbourne, VIC 3207, Australia

314–321, 3rd Floor, Plot 3, Splendor Forum, Jasola District Centre, New Delhi – 110025, India

103 Penang Road, #05-06/07, Visioncrest Commercial, Singapore 238467

Cambridge University Press is part of the University of Cambridge.

It furthers the University's mission by disseminating knowledge in the pursuit of education, learning and research at the highest international levels of excellence.

www.cambridge.org
Information on this title: www.cambridge.org/9781108799027

© Cambridge University Press 2021

First published 2021

20 19 18 17 16 15 14 13 12 11 10 9 8

Printed in Poland by Opolgraf

A catalogue record for this publication is available from the British Library

ISBN 978-1-108-79902-7 Workbook with Digital Access (1 Year)

Cambridge International copyright material in this publication is reproduced under license and remains the intellectual property of Cambridge Assessment International Education

⟩ Contents

English Skills and Support

1 Cells

2 Materials and their structure

7 Microorganisms in the environment

8 Changes to materials

9 Electricity

> How to use this book

This workbook will help you to use and understand the English that is involved while learning science.

It will help you to:

- understand what you read in your science books, and what your teacher tells you during the lessons

- talk to other learners in your class in English, during your science lessons, using the correct vocabulary

- understand questions that you are asked by your teacher or in a test

- speak or write answers to science questions that say clearly what you mean.

This workbook contains an **English Skills and Support** section. This contains information about English grammar and vocabulary to help you with science. You can use the reference section at any time you need help with English while studying science.

Singular and plural verbs

A verb is a word that describes an action or state.

The verb to be
The verb *to be* includes am, is and are. They are used with other verbs and must agree with what or who you are talking about. For example: *I am, he is, we are.*

Who or what	verb to be	noun
I	am	a scientist.
She	is	a student.
We	are	biologists.

The verb *is* can be used with singular things. For example: There *is a* reaction.

The verb *are* is used with plural things. For example: There *are many* organs in the human body.

When you use other verbs, they have to agree with the person or object you are talking about.

This workbook provides questions for you to practise what you have learned in class. There is a topic to match each topic in your Learner's Book and Exercises in each Topic. You can use the English Skills and Support section to help you as you complete the Exercises.

Exercise 1 Singular and plural

This exercise gives you practice in using singular and plural forms of verbs.

Look at **Singular and plural verbs** in the *English Language Skills and Support* section for information about singular and plural verbs.

Circle the word that best completes each of these sentences.

a   A liquid **take** / **takes** the shape of the container it is in.

b   Gases **are** / **is** easy to compress.

c   Particle theory **explains** / **explain** the properties of the three states of matter.

d   The arrangement of particles **is** / **are** different in solids, liquids and gases.

Exercise 2 Properties

In this exercise, you will think about the properties of solids, liquids and gases.

> English Skills and Support

This book is to help you with English skills when you are studying science. The *English Skills and Support* section gives you information about important topics in English that you will use in science. You can use this section at any time you need help with English while studying science.

In this section, there is information about English grammar and vocabulary to help you with science.

You will see many different grammatical words in the English skills and support section explained. This first part shows you some basic information that will help you.

Quick reference guide

Grammar	Use	Example
Noun	a name of an object, person or animal	a tripod, Marcus, a cat
Verb	a word that describes an action or state	(to) mix, do, melt, write, carry
Adjective	a word that describes a noun	the **blue** book; the **soft** material

Singular and plural nouns

Singular means one thing.

Plural means two or more things.

A **noun** is the name of an object, person or animal.

You can add **s** to the end of many English nouns to make them plural.

+s	
Singular	Plural
cell	cell**s**
organ	organ**s**
experiment	experiment**s**

Example sentences:

> A **heart** is an **organ**.
>
> There are many **organs** in a human **body**.

For nouns ending in s, ss, sh, ch, x or z add **es**: Notice that some English words end in s, but they are singular.

+es	
Singular	Plural
lens	lens**es**
mass	mass**es**
dish	dish**es**
bench	bench**es**
box	box**es**
quiz	quiz**zes**

Example sentences:

> The microscope has a good **lens**.
>
> The **lenses** in our glasses help us see better.

For nouns ending in consonant +y, remove the -y and add **ies** to make it plural. Vowels are the letters a, e, i, o and u. All other letters are consonants.

+ies	
Singular	Plural
activity	activit**ies**
fly	fl**ies**
theory	theor**ies**

Example sentences:

> I will use English in this **activity**.
>
> We do many **activities** in science lessons.

For nouns ending in vowel + y, just add **s** to make it plural. Remember, vowels are the letters a, e, i, o and u.

+s	
Singular	Plural
key	keys
ray	rays

Some nouns describe things that are countable, which means that you can count them.

'Countable' nouns	
Singular	Plural
beaker	beakers
tripod	tripods
thermometer	thermometers

Example sentence:

> I need more **beakers**. Can you pass me that **beaker**, please?

Some nouns describe things that are uncountable, which means that you cannot count them.

For example, air, bread and iron are usually uncountable.

'Uncountable' nouns
water
oxygen
sodium chloride

Example sentence:

> All of the beakers contain **water**.

Unusual singular and plural nouns

A lot of English words come from other languages. Many science words come from the Latin and ancient Greek languages. This makes the plural forms unusual.

Latin and ancient Greek words			
ending in...		change to...	
singular		plural	
-a	alga	-ae	algae
-um	bacterium	-a	bacteria
-us	fungus	-i	fungi
-on	mitochondrion	-a	mitochondria

Singular and plural verbs

A **verb** is a word that describes an action or state.

The verb *to be*

The verb *to be* includes am, is and are. They are used with other verbs and must agree with what or who you are talking about. For example: *I am*, *he is*, *we are*.

Who or what	verb to be	noun
I	am	a scientist.
She	is	a student.
We	are	biologists.

The verb *is* can be used with singular things. For example: There *is* a reaction.

The verb *are* is used with plural things. For example: There *are many* organs in the human body.

When you use other verbs, they have to agree with the person or object you are talking about.

Verbs

Who or what	Verbs
I, you, we, they	mix, experiment, discover, look, use
It, she, he	mixes, experiments, discovers, looks, uses

When you start a sentence with *it*, *she* or *he*, you must put an -s or -es on the end of the verb.

Note that the verb can be followed by a singular or plural noun, for example: He discovers a solution, or, he discovers solutions.

In summary, it is easy to get confused with the letter -s at the ends of English words.

Remember: an -s or -es on the end of a noun usually makes it plural (for example: 1 pen, 2 *pens*).

Remember: an -s or -es on the end of most verbs makes it agree with it, she, he. (for example: it *boils*, she *mixes*).

Connecting words

Connecting words help you to join two pieces of information together.

We can join two things together with connecting words, for example: *and*, *but*, *because*. These are called **connectives**. Connectives are like glue – they stick two ideas together.

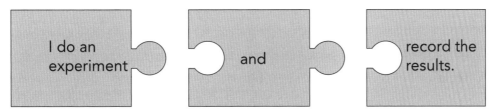

There are many connecting words in English and they do different things in sentences.

Connective		What it is used for
and	→	connects two positive things together
but	→	connects a positive and a negative thing together
because	→	gives a reason why

Here are some examples.

and		positive	+	positive
		Iron is strong	and	magnetic.
but		positive	+	negative
		Copper is malleable	but	it is not magnetic.
because		fact or situation	+	why
		Stainless steel is used for knives and forks	because	it doesn't rust.

Comparative and superlative adjectives

An adjective describes a noun.

Adjective	Noun
blue	paper
hot	liquid
small	bird

Comparative adjectives show the differences between things.

Superlative adjectives say what is at the top and the bottom of a range, or the extremes.

In science, you often want to **describe** things.

Adjectives are words that describe someone or something.

Examples of adjectives:

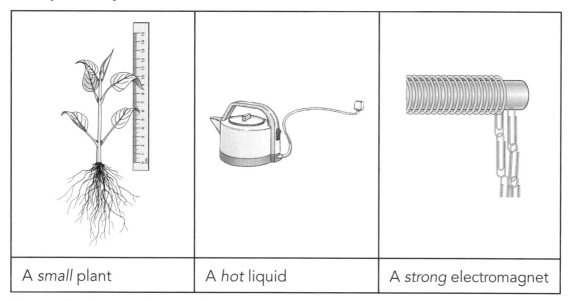

| A *small* plant | A *hot* liquid | A *strong* electromagnet |

Some adjectives are short and some are long. Short adjectives have one syllable (sound). Long adjectives have three syllables (sounds) or more. Adjectives with two syllables that end in 'y' follow the short adjective rules. Adjectives with two syllables that do not end in 'y' follow the long adjective rules.

Short adjectives	Long adjectives
big, small, hot, cold, strong, weak	flexible, acidic, magnetic, powerful

Comparative and superlative adjectives work a little differently with short and long adjectives.

This is how they work with short adjectives.

Comparative adjectives			Superlative adjectives		
You make a comparative adjective by adding *-er* to the end of a short adjective.			You make a superlative adjective by adding 'the' before the adjective and by adding -est to the end of short adjectives.		
Adjective		Comparative	Adjective		Superlative
cold		colder	cold		the coldest
small	+er →	smaller	small	+est →	the smallest
long		longer	long		the longest

For example:

- Ice is colder than water.
- Ice is the coldest.

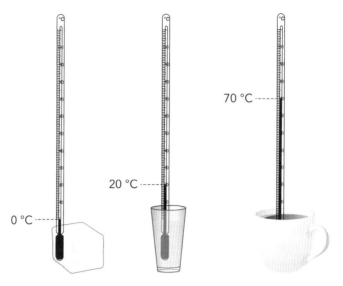

This is how comparatives and superlatives work with long adjectives:

Comparative adjectives		
You make a comparative adjective by adding **more** before a long adjective.		
adjective	more	complete comparative
flexible		more flexible
acidic	+ more	more acidic
powerful		more powerful

Superlative adjectives		
You make a superlative adjective by adding **the most** before a long adjective.		
adjective	the most	complete superlative
flexible		the most flexible
acidic	+ the most	the most acidic
powerful		the most powerful

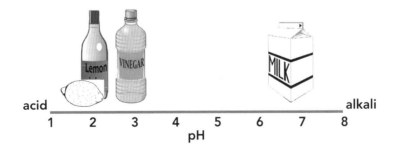

For example:

- Vinegar is more acidic than milk.
- Lemon juice is the most acidic liquid.

Notice that you always put *the* before a superlative adjective. To make comparatives and superlatives for 'less' rather than 'more', you add the word 'less' before the adjective to make a comparative adjective, and 'the least' before the adjective to make a superlative adjective.

Be careful! Words with two syllables (sounds) can be both *-er* and *more*. For two-syllable adjectives ending in -y add -er. Notice that the spelling changes when you take off the -y, you add *-ier*.

For example:

- This oil is greasy.

- Oil is greasier than gel.

- Oil is the greasiest liquid.

Two-syllable adjectives – ending in -y		
Adjective	Comparative adjective	Superlative adjective
cloudy	cloudier	the cloudiest
easy	easier	the easiest
greasy	greasier	the greasiest

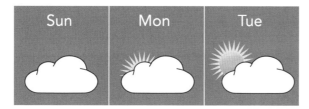

For example:

- Monday was <u>cloudier</u> than Tuesday.

- Sunday was <u>the cloudiest</u> day.

For two-syllable adjectives **not** ending in -y add *more* before the adjective.

Two-syllable adjectives – not ending in -y		
Adjective	Comparative adjective	Superlative adjectives
important	**more** important	**the most** important
active	**more** active	**the most** active
distant	**more** distant	**the most** distant

For example:

*   Jupiter is **more distant** from the Sun than Earth is from the Sun.

*   Neptune is **the most distant** planet from the Sun.

There are always exceptions to the rule! There are some irregular adjectives that don't follow the usual pattern. The adjective *bad* changes to *worse* in the comparative form and *the worst* in the superlative form. The adjective *good* changes to *better* in the comparative form and *the best* in the superlative form.

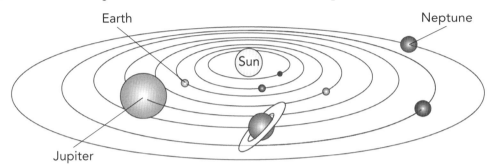

Adjective	Comparative adjective	Superlative adjective
bad	worse	the worst
	For example: The results were **worse** than expected.	For example: This method is **the worst**.
good	better	the best
	For example: The results of the second experiment were <u>better</u> than those of the first one.	For example: These results were **the best**.

You can also use adjectives to talk about things that are the same.

To talk about things that are alike, you can say: As one thing increases, another thing also increases by using '*the more... the more*'.

You can either use a noun or a verb after 'the more.'

The more + noun, the more + noun.
The more mass an object has, the more friction there is.
The more + verb, the more + verb.
The more polluted the air is, the more unhealthy the people are.

For example: **The more** heat there is, **the more** energy it has.

You can use *more, less, greater* or *smaller* to show the effect of one action on another.

For example: The **more** matter an object contains, the **greater** its mass.

You can also use *as much as* or *not as much as*.

Example:					
Leaf A	is	as	long	as	Leaf B.
Form:					
Object 1	is	as	adjective	as	object 2.

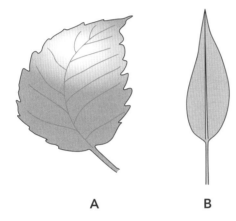

A   B

For example: I exercise **as much as** my friend. Notice that a verb is used before 'as much as' in this sentence.

Question words

In science you will often ask questions. It is important to use the correct question word to get the information you need.

Question word	is used to...	Example sentence
Who	talk about people	Who is doing the experiment?
Where	talk about a place	Where is the tripod?
When	talk about a time	When can we start the activity?
Why	ask for an explanation or reason	Why is the sky blue?
What	ask for information	What is this called?
Which	make a choice	Which chemical do I use?

Command words

Science questions often start with *name, explain* or *describe*. You need to know how to answer questions of this type correctly.

Command words	Answer
Name	Give the **name** of the person, object or animal.
Explain	Say **why** something happens.
Describe	Say **what** happens.

For example:

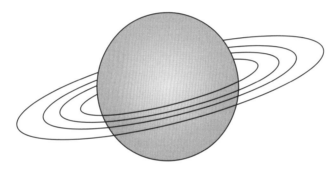

Question: **Name** the planet.

Answer: Saturn

Question: **Describe** how particles are arranged in a solid.

Answer: In solids the particles are arranged in a fixed pattern. The particles are held together strongly and are tightly packed together.

Question: **Explain** why liquids cannot change volume.

Answer: Matter can only change volume if the particles in it can spread out or move closer together. In a liquid, the particles are very close together and cannot be compressed (pushed closer together). The particles touch each other but they can move past each other.

Active and passive

You will see sentences using **active verbs** and **passive verbs** in science. Sometimes you need to use passive verbs, but active sentences are easier to understand.

Active verbs

Use active verbs in sentences to give direct and clear information.

Structure: Who *does* / *did* what.

Examples:

* I learn science.

* I mixed the chemicals.

Passive verbs

Passive sentences are not as direct.

Structure: Something is / are / was / were done by someone or something.

Example:

* Water **is boiled** by heating it.

* Goggles and gloves **are worn** in the laboratory.

Changing active to passive

Tense		Active	
	Who / what	verb	
Simple present	I, you, we, they	**record**	the results.
Simple present	She, he, it	**records**	the results.

Passive sentences often do not say who or what carried out the action.

Form of the verb		Passive
	What	is / are + past participle
Past participle	The result	**is recorded**
Past participle	The results	**are recorded**

Notice how the word order changes when you change active to passive.

Word order

There are many ways to write sentences in English. The order of words in a sentence depends on the grammar used and what you want to say.

Let's start with positive (+), negative (−) and question (?) forms in sentences.

	Who/what	verb	extra information
+	Water	boils	at 100 degrees Celsius.
+	I	draw	the graph.

	Who/what	verb	negative	verb	extra information
−	Water	does	not	boil	at 80 degrees Celsius.
−	I	do	not	draw	graphs.

	Question word	who/what	verb	extra information
?	Does	water	boil	at 100 degrees Celsius?
?	Do	I	draw	the graph?

Notice that the question word goes first in a question form.

Modal verbs

Modal verbs show that things are **possible, probable** or **certain**.

Modal verbs can also be used to make **suggestions, recommendations** and **predictions**.

In science, you often want to say if something is certain, probable, possible or impossible.

Modal verbs are a special type of verb that go before normal verbs in a sentence. Modal verbs add meaning to verbs.

There are many modal verbs and each one has a different job or jobs.

Here are some of the common modal verbs:

Can	In this example, this modal verb shows: an **ability** to do something
A battery **can** power a toy. (A battery *has the ability to* power the toy.)	
Cannot / can't	This means the opposite. It means: you are **not able** to do something
Arun **can't** lift the heavy weight. (In this example, Arun *does **not** have the ability* to lift the weight.)	

Must	This is a strong modal verb and it means that something is essential to do.
You **must** breathe air to live. (It is essential for life.)	
Must not / mustn't	This means the opposite. It means that it is essential **not** to do something.
You **must not** mix potassium with acid. (It is essential **not** to do this as it is very dangerous.)	

Should	Use this modal verb to: • give **advice** • make a **recommendation**.
You **should** prepare equipment carefully before doing an experiment. (I suggest that you do this).	
Should not / shouldn't	This means the opposite. It means: • give advice **not** to do something • something is **not** recommended.
You **shouldn't** use a dirty beaker when doing an experiment. (I suggest that you do **not** do this).	

Making predictions

In science, you often want to guess what will happen at the end of an experiment before you have done it.

You can use *will* to talk about the future.

For example: 'I **will** go to school tomorrow.'

You can also use *will* to talk about future predictions. What you think **will** happen.

For example:

Will	This modal verb shows future possibility
I think the metal **will** rust.	

Another way to predict what will happen in the future, is to say:
If *A* happens, *B* will be the result.

For example:

If and will	This shows prediction/cause and effect.
If you put the iron nail in water and air, it **will** rust. (If you decide to do this experiment, this is what I think will happen.)	

Notice that a sentence with *if* has two halves. Each half is called a **clause**.

You can write the sentence starting with the *if clause* or the *result clause*.

For example:

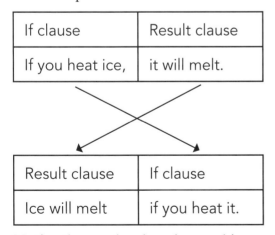

If clause	Result clause
If you heat ice,	it will melt.

Result clause	If clause
Ice will melt	if you heat it.

Notice the word order when making predictions can change.

When you start with the *if clause*, you use a comma (,) at the end of the clause.
When you start with the *result clause*, you don't need to use a comma.

Also note that *if* and *whether* are very similar.

Use *if* when you have a conditional sentence.

Use *whether* when you are showing that two alternatives are possible.

If we heat a gas, it will expand.

I don't know whether milk is an acid or an alkali.

Results tables

You need to know the names for the different parts of tables. The words you need to know are *column, row* and *heading*.

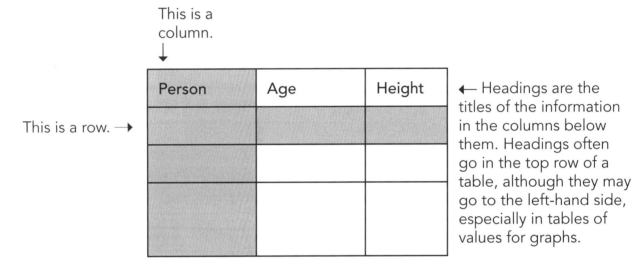

This is a
column.
↓

Person	Age	Height

This is a row. →

← Headings are the titles of the information in the columns below them. Headings often go in the top row of a table, although they may go to the left-hand side, especially in tables of values for graphs.

Observations and conclusions

In science you will make observations and conclusions. It is important to know the difference between them because they can easily be confused.

An **observation** is something that you notice. You use your senses to make an observation. You can use sight, smell, touch or hearing.

A **conclusion** is something that you work out from the results of your experiment.

In science, you often **observe** and then make a **conclusion.** For example:

Sofia observes that there is more mould on the orange kept in the warm room than in the fridge.

She concludes that mould grows more quickly at higher temperatures.

Using prepositions with verbs

Phrasal verbs are made up of a verb followed by a preposition. Prepositions are usually short words, for example: *in, on, at, by, from*. Phrasal verbs are used a lot in English and science. Phrasal verbs can have many meanings, but these are the common uses of them in science.

Verbs used without a preposition have one meaning but, when you add a preposition to the verb, it has a different meaning. *Carry* and *carry out* are used a lot in science, so it is important to know the difference.

It is easy to work out some phrasal verbs, for example, 'The lights reflect off the mirror.' Off here means the light bounces away from the surface of the mirror. Other phrasal verbs are not as easy to understand the meaning, for example. 'To carry out experiments.'

Verb	Preposition	Meaning	Example
Carry		To transport	The wind carries seeds through the air.
Carry	out	To do	I carry out experiments.
Take	in	To use, eat, absorb	Plants need to take in water, sunlight and nutrients to grow.
Mix	up	To confuse	Don't mix up observations with conclusions.
Find	out	To research, to discover information or a result	I need to find out the acidity of lemon juice.
Run	out	To have nothing left/ to have used it all up	I have run out of paper.
Work	out	To solve a problem/ to find the answer to a problem	I have worked out why this gas burns.

Language for planning experiments

When you are planning experiments, you need to know some important words. A **variable** is something that can change. You also need to know what **dependent variables, independent variables** and a **fair test** are.

The **independent variable** is the variable that you change during a scientific experiment.

The **dependent variable** is the variable that changes, when you change the independent variable during a scientific experiment.

A **fair test** is one in which only one variable is changed at a time, so that you can be sure what caused the change in the dependent variable (the variable being tested).

This is the end of the *English Skills and Support Section*. Remember, the English information is to help you with the science exercises that follow. You can look back at this section and revisit the English information at any time.

1 ▸ Cells

❯ 1.1 Plant Cells

Exercise 1 Parts of a plant cell

> This exercise gives you practice in writing the names of the parts of a plant cell.

The diagram shows a plant cell.

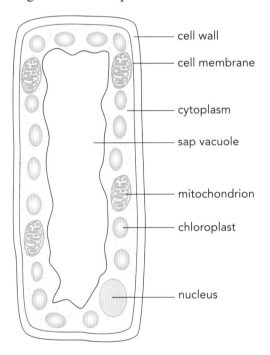

cell wall

cell membrane

cytoplasm

sap vacuole

mitochondrion

chloroplast

nucleus

Complete each of the following sentences. Use the words from the diagram labels. Use each word once.

Make sure that you spell each word correctly.

a   The layer on the outside of a plant cell is called the cell ....

b   The thin layer between the cell wall and the cytoplasm is the cell

    ....

c   The clear jelly that fills most of a cell is called ....

d   The large space inside the cell is the ....

     It contains ....

e   The round, dark structure inside the cytoplasm is the ....

f   The small oval structures inside the cytoplasm are ....

g   The cytoplasm also contains ....

Exercise 2 Singular and plural nouns

This exercise is about writing sentences about one or many things.

Look at **Singular and plural nouns** in the *English Language Skills and Support* section for information about singular and plural nouns.

- The plural of mitochondrion is mitochondria.

- Nucleus ends with -s, but it is a singular word. The plural of nucleus is nuclei.

- Cellulose, cytoplasm and chlorophyll are 'uncountable' nouns.

Circle the correct word to complete each sentence.

a   The singular of mitochondria is **mitochondrion** / **mitochondrias** / **mitochondri**.

b   Each cell contains only one **nuclei** / **nucleus** / **nucleuses** but may have many chloroplasts.

c   All cell walls contain **cellulose** / **celluloses** / **cellulos**.

d   Chloroplasts contain **chlorophylli** / **chlorophylls** / **chlorophyll**.

Exercise 3 Limitations

No one is perfect. We all have limitations. A limitation is something that we cannot do absolutely perfectly. This exercise will help you to use the word correctly.

Marcus uses a microscope to look at plant cells.

Marcus writes some sentences about using the microscope.

Tick (✓) each sentence that describes a **limitation** of the microscope that he uses.

The microscope gives a clear picture of the cells. ☐

The microscope only works well when I place it next to the window. ☐

The microscope does not magnify the cells as much as I want it to. ☐

The microscope is easy to use. ☐

> 1.2 Animal cells

Exercise 1 Using connecting words

In this exercise, you will practise using connecting words. This will also help you to remember the similarities and differences between animal cells and plant cells.

Look at **Connecting words** in the *English Language Skills and Support* section for information about connecting words.

Complete each sentence. Choose the best word from these three:

and   because   but

a   All plant cells have a cell wall .... animal cells do not.

b   An animal cell has a cell membrane .... a plant cell also has one.

c   Every cell needs a nucleus .... this controls the activities of the cell.

d   Both animal cells .... plant cells have cytoplasm.

Exercise 2 Describing an activity

You can give instructions to someone else to help them to do an activity.
You need to make the instructions clear and simple. In this exercise, you will
think about the best sequence (order) for a set of instructions.

Zara wants to know how to use a microscope to look at animal cells. Sofia gives her
instructions. The instructions are in the wrong order.

A   Put the slide onto the stage of the microscope.

B   Add a blue stain to the cells.

C   Put a coverslip over the stained cells.

D   Put some animal cells onto a clean microscope slide.

E   Focus the microscope so that you can see the cells.

Write the letters of the instructions in the correct sequence.

> 1.3 Specialised cells

Exercise 1 Describing functions

> The function of something is a useful thing that it does. The function of this book is to help you to use English in your science work. One function of your brain is to think. This exercise will help you to describe the functions of some specialised cells.

Here is a list of the functions of some specialised cells.

move mucus up and away from the lungs

make food by photosynthesis

absorb water and minerals from the soil

transport oxygen around the body

carry electrical signals

Use the list to help you to complete these sentences. Copy the words carefully and try not to make any spelling mistakes.

a   **The function of** a red blood cell is to ....

    ....

b   **The function of** a ciliated cell is to ....

    ....

c   **The function of** a root hair cell is to ....

    ....

d   **The function of** a neurone is to ....

    ....

e   **The function of** a palisade cell is to ....

    ....

Exercise 2 Carry and carry out

In this exercise, you will practise using the verbs 'carry' and 'carry out' correctly.

The verb 'carry' means 'transport'. But 'carry out' means do. For example:

- We carry out an experiment.

- A cell carries out its functions.

- You carry out your teacher's instructions.

Complete these sentences. Choose from these words. You can use each word once, more than once or not at all.

carry   carry out

a   Red blood cells are specialised to be able to ………………………… oxygen

around the body. To help them to ………………………… this function, they

contain a red pigment called haemoglobin.

b   Neurones ………………………… electrical signals from one part of the body to

another. Each neurone has a long axon and many small dendrites. These help

them to ………………………… their function.

c   Ciliated cells ………………………… the function of keeping the lungs clean.

They have cilia that sweep mucus upwards, to ………………………… dust and

bacteria away from the lungs.

> 1.4 Cells, tissues and organs

Exercise 1 Avoiding the word 'it'.

> You have to be very careful when using the word 'it'. Sometimes, it is not clear what 'it' refers to. It is often a good idea not to use 'it' but to use the correct word instead.

Zara writes some sentences about cells, tissues and organs. Her teacher says that she is not sure that all the sentences are correct, because she does not know what 'it' refers to.

For each of these sentences, decide what Zara should write instead of 'it'. Underline your choice.

a   A leaf is an organ that has an upper epidermis. It carries out photosynthesis.

   In this sentence, 'it' means **the leaf / the upper epidermis**.

b   A tissue is a group of similar cells, such as the palisade layer in a leaf. It can be part of an organ.

   In this sentence, 'it' means **a tissue / the palisade layer**.

c   A person is an organism containing many organ systems, such as the circulatory system. It transports substances around the body.

   In this sentence, 'it' means **a person / an organism / the circulatory system**.

Exercise 2 Vocabulary practice

This exercise will help you to remember the meanings of some of the new words you have covered in this topic.

Draw a line to match each word with its meaning.

Word	Meaning

| spongy layer | a group of organs working together to carry out a function |

| ciliated epithelium | a tissue found in animals but not in plants, which helps to sweep mucus up from the lungs |

| lower epidermis | the layer of cells that covers the underside of a plant leaf |

| onion epidermis | a tissue made up of cells containing chloroplasts, with large air spaces between the cells |

| organ | a structure made up of several different types of tissue |

| organ system | a tissue that covers each layer inside an onion bulb |

2 ▶ Materials and their structure

> 2.1 Solids, liquids and gases

Exercise 1 Singular and plural

> This exercise gives you practice in using singular and plural forms of verbs.

> Look at **Singular and plural verbs** in the *English Language Skills and Support* section for information about singular and plural verbs.

Ⓒircle the word that best completes each of these sentences.

a   A liquid **take** / **takes** the shape of the container it is in.

b   Gases **are** / **is** easy to compress.

c   Particle theory **explains** / **explain** the properties of the three states of matter.

d   The arrangement of particles **is** / **are** different in solids, liquids and gases.

Exercise 2 Properties

> In this exercise, you will think about the properties of solids, liquids and gases.

> In everyday language, a property is something that is yours. The pen you are writing with is your property. In science, you can also use the word 'property' to mean a feature or characteristic of something.

Complete this table by writing these words or phrases in the correct places. There are two possible places for two of the phrases.

- **state of matter**
- **property**
- **keeps the same shape**
- **fills its container**
- **can be compressed**
- **can be poured**

....	....		
	solid	liquid	gas
....	✓		
....		✓	✓
....			✓
....			✓

Exercise 3 Vocabulary practice

This exercise gives you more practice in using the vocabulary in this topic.

Complete the sentences by using some of the words from the list.

compress	flow	liquid	particle	particles
properties	spaces	vacuum	vibrate	volume

a   It is easy to change the .... of a gas, but not a solid.

b   In a gas, the .... are a long way apart.

c   The particles in a solid .... in the same place.

d   There are no particles in a ....

e   Liquids can .... from one place to another.

f   The .... theory helps to explain the .... of the three states of matter.

› 2.2 Changes of state

Exercise 1 Boiling and evaporation

> This exercise asks you to think carefully about the similarities and differences between boiling and evaporation. You will practise using suitable words to describe these two processes.

The words **steam** and **water vapour** can both be used to mean water in the form of a gas. Generally, you use **steam** when the gas is very hot, and **water vapour** when it is the same temperature as the air around it.

Complete the sentences about boiling and evaporation. Choose words and phrases from the list.

boiling	**changes of state**	**condensation**	**evaporation**
fastest	**gas**	**liquid**	**slowest**
solid	**steam**	**water vapour**	

Boiling and evaporation are both .... In both

boiling and evaporation, a .... changes

to a ....

The particles in a liquid are always moving. Some particles move faster than others.

Even when the liquid is quite cold, some of the ....

particles escape and fly off to form a gas. This gas is called ....

This process is called ....

If you heat the liquid, it can reach a temperature at which all the particles are

moving so fast that the whole liquid starts to turn into a gas. This temperature is

called the .... point of the liquid. The hot gas is called

....

Exercise 2 Making predictions

In this exercise, you will practise using the word 'if' to make predictions. A prediction says what you think will happen.

Look at **Making predictions** in the *English Language Skills and Support* section for information about making predictions.

Each of these sentences contains a prediction. The words are mixed up.

Put the words in the correct order to make sentences.

Remember to use a capital letter (A) and a full stop (.) for each of your sentences.

a   will liquid if a boil you enough heat it.

    ....

b   cool if a liquid it freeze you will enough

    ....

c   you condense will if cool gas it a

    ....

d   a it if melt you heat melting solid will its point to

    ....

Exercise 3 Naming and using scientific apparatus

It is important to know and use the correct names for scientific apparatus. This exercise checks that you know the names and uses of five pieces of apparatus.

a   Look at the pictures of apparatus.

Add a number to the Diagram of apparatus and Use boxes that matches the correct number next to the name of each piece of apparatus.

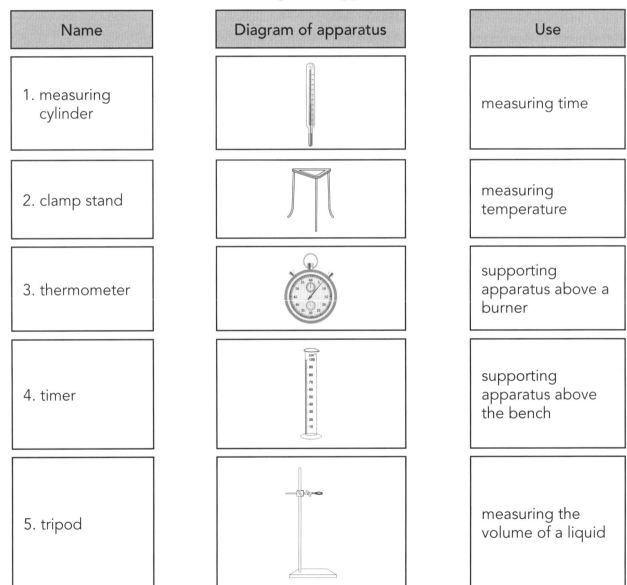

Name	Diagram of apparatus	Use
1. measuring cylinder		measuring time
2. clamp stand		measuring temperature
3. thermometer		supporting apparatus above a burner
4. timer		supporting apparatus above the bench
5. tripod		measuring the volume of a liquid

b Complete the sentences about using apparatus correctly. The missing words are not all taken from part **a** of this execise.

When you read a volume on a measuring cylinder, read the scale at

the bottom of the m.......................... . Make sure that your eyes

are l........................ with the m......................... .

When you want to find the boiling point of a liquid, heat it until it is boiling

vig......................... Then use a t......................... to measure the

temperature.

> 2.3 Explaining changes of state

Exercise 1 The more..., the more...

In this exercise, you will practise using a sentence structure that we often use in science.

Look at **Comparative and Superlative Adjectives** in the *English Language Skills and Support* section for general information about sentence structure.

Complete each of the following sentences.

Use these words:

more   **less**

a   The more you heat a solid, the .... space its particles take up.

b   The more you heat a solid, the .... energy the particles have.

c   The more you heat a liquid, the .... the particles move.

d   The more you cool a liquid, the .... energy its particles have.

e   The more you heat a gas, the .... volume it takes up.

f   The more you cool a gas, the .... quickly its particles move.

Exercise 2 Vocabulary practice

This exercise gives you more practice in using some of the scientific terms in this topic.

Which word or phrase fits each of these descriptions?

Choose from these words.

attractive forces	boil	condense	evaporating	expand
fixed pattern	freeze	heat energy	melt	transferred

a   You use this word to describe the 'movement' of heat energy from one thing to another, for example, from a burner to a solid.

   ....

b   This word means changing from a liquid to a gas, while the liquid is at a temperature below its boiling point.

   ....

c   These words describe what holds particles together in a solid.

   ....

d   This word describes what happens to a solid when you heat it, and its particles take up more space.

   ....

e   These words describe the arrangement of the particles in a solid.

   ....

> 2.4 The water cycle

Exercise 1 Describe and explain

In science, questions often ask you to 'describe' something or 'explain' something. This exercise gives you practice in giving the correct kind of answer for each of these command words.

Look at **command words** in the *English Language Skills and Support* section for information about command words.

This flow diagram shows part of the water cycle.

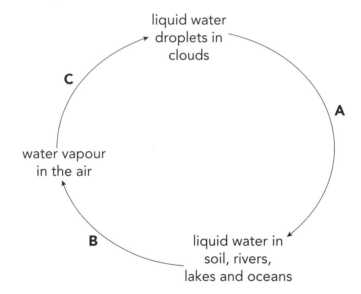

Here are some questions that Marcus answers.

Questions

Describe what is shown by arrow A.

Explain what happens at A.

Describe what happens at B.

Explain what happens at B.

Describe what happens at C.

Explain what happens at C.

Here are the answers that Marcus writes.

Write the question that Marcus is answering above his answer.

Answers

a ....

Water evaporates.

b ....

The fastest-moving particles in the water escape into the air as gas, so the water changes into water vapour.

c ....

The water vapour condenses to form liquid water.

d ....

Precipitation – rain and snow.

e ....

The water vapour cools as it rises up in the air. The particles in the water vapour get closer together and the gas changes into a liquid. The tiny droplets of liquid water form clouds.

f ....

The tiny droplets of water in the clouds join together to make raindrops, which fall to the ground.

Exercise 2 Water cycle vocabulary

This exercise gives you more practice in using words that describe different parts of the water cycle.

Draw **one** line to match a description to the correct word.

Description		Word
water that soaks into the soil and rocks		precipitation
water that flows across the ground and into lakes, rivers and the sea		groundwater
the loss of water vapour from the leaves of plants		surface run-off
water falling as snow, rain, hail or sleet		transpiration

› 2.5 Atoms, elements and the Periodic Table

Exercise 1 Comparatives and superlatives

In this exercise you will practise using words that describe differences between things.

Look at **Comparative and superlative adjectives** in the *English Language Skills and Support* section for information about comparatives and superlatives – talking about differences and extremes.

This diagram shows part of the Periodic Table.

☐ metals																	
☐ non-metals				H hydrogen													He helium
Li lithium	Be beryllium										B boron	C carbon	N nitrogen	O oxygen	F fluorine	Ne neon	
Na sodium	Mg magnesium										Al aluminium	Si silicon	P phosphorus	S sulfur	Cl chlorine	Ar argon	
K potassium	Ca calcium																

a Which element in the Periodic Table has atoms with the smallest mass?

....

b Do atoms of magnesium have a larger or smaller mass than atoms of sodium?

....

c What is the symbol of the element in the third group that has atoms with the largest mass?

....

d Does an atom of nitrogen have a larger or smaller mass than an atom of phosphorus?

....

e Does an atom of boron have a larger or smaller mass than an atom of argon?

....

f Which elements in the diagram have atoms with a larger mass than atoms of chlorine?

....

g Which element in the same period as carbon has atoms with the smallest mass?

....

h What is the symbol of the metal that has atoms with the smallest mass?

....

i Which non-metals have atoms with a larger mass than the atoms of sodium?

....

> 2.6 Compounds and formulae

Exercise 1 Naming compounds

It is important to write the names of compounds correctly. This exercise will help you to check that you can get these names right.

1 Circle the correct name for each of these compounds.

a A compound formed when sodium and chlorine combine.

chloride	chlorine	sodium	sodium
sodium	sodium	chloride	chlorine

b The compound with the formula H_2S.

hydrogen	hydrogen	sulfur	sulfur
sulfide	sulfur	hydride	hydrogen

c The compound with the formula H_2O.

dihydrogen	hydrogen	hydrogen	water
oxide	dioxide	oxide	

d A compound of carbon and oxygen that contains the same number of carbon atoms as oxygen atoms.

carbon	carbon	monocarbon	oxygen
monoxide	oxide	oxide	carbide

Exercise 2 Connecting words

This exercise provides practice in using the best connecting word to link two ideas.

Complete the sentences by using these connecting words:

and	because	but

a   The formula for carbon dioxide is CO_2 .... it contains

   one atom of carbon .... two atoms of oxygen
   combined together.

b   Sodium is a very reactive element .... when it combines
   with chlorine it forms a much less reactive compound.

c   Magnesium oxide contains magnesium .... oxygen
   combined together.

d   The name of a compound is written in words ....
   the formula uses symbols.

e   Elements are made of a single kind of atom ....
   compounds are made of two or more kinds of atom bonded together.

> 2.7 Compounds and mixtures

Exercise 1 Using active and passive verbs

This exercise helps you to use active and passive verbs. Often, it is better to use an active verb. This is easier to do and it can make your meaning clearer.

Look at **Active and passive verbs** in the *English Language Skills and Support* section for information about active and passive verbs.

These sentences each use a passive verb.

Use an active form of the same verb to complete the sentences.

The first one has been done for you.

a Six elements **are shown** in the list.

   The list **shows** six elements.

b The water **is evaporated** off by heating.

   Heating .... off the water.

c A mixture **is made up** of different kinds of particles.

   Many kinds of particles .... a mixture.

d Several different gases **are contained** in air.

   Air .... several different gases.

e Iron filings and sulfur **are heated** together by the teacher.

   The teacher .... iron filings and sulfur together.

f Only water **is contained** in pure water.

   Pure water .... only water.

Exercise 2 Naming and using scientific apparatus

This is another opportunity to make sure that you can use the correct names for some pieces of scientific apparatus.

Here are some pictures of apparatus that you can use to find out what a water sample contains.

Draw lines from each piece of apparatus to its name and its use.

Name	Diagram of apparatus	Use
evaporating basin		container for a liquid – you can heat and evaporate water from it
tongs		supporting an evaporating dish
pipe-clay triangle		safely holding something hot
safety glasses		protecting your eyes from splashes
tripod		supporting apparatus above a burner

3 ▶ Forces and energy

> 3.1 Gravity, weight and mass

Exercise 1 Connecting words

> This exercise provides practice in using the best connecting word to link two ideas.

Complete the sentences by using these connecting words:

and   **because**   **but**

a   We do not fall off the surface of the Earth ……………………… the gravity of the Earth is strong.

b   Weight is measured in newtons ……………………… mass is measured in kg.

c   The chair does not fall through the floor ……………………… the floor pushes up on the chair with a force equal to its weight.

d   Weight ……………………… strength of gravity on Mercury are much less than they are on Earth.

e   If you travel to a planet with gravity larger than the gravity of Earth, your

   mass stays the same ……………………… your weight increases.

Exercise 2 Vocabulary practice

Doing this exercise will help you check that you can use the words and phrases about gravity, weight and mass correctly.

Complete each sentence by using some of the following words and phrases. You can use each one once, more than once or not at all.

pulls away from the centre   **acts towards the centre**

formula triangle   **gravity**   **mass**   **properly**

accurately   **quantity**   **weight**   **contact force**

a   You need to use a good-quality force meter, and read the scale carefully,

   to make sure you measure the weight ....

b   The pull of gravity .... of the Earth.

c   You can use a .... to see how to calculate any of the
   three quantities in an equation.

d   Arun doesn't fall through the chair because the ....
   from the chair is equal to his weight.

e   Mass is the .... of matter in an object.

> 3.2 Formation of the Solar System

Exercise 1 Using active and passive verbs

This exercise helps you to use active and passive verbs. Often, it is better to use an active verb. This is easier to do and it can make your meaning clearer.

Look at **Active and passive verbs** in the *English Language Skills and Support* section for information about active and passive verbs.

These sentences each use a passive verb.

Complete the sentences by using an active form of the same verb.

The first one has been done for you.

a   The rock **is pulled** towards the centre of the Earth by gravity.

Gravity **pulls** the rock towards the centre of the Earth.

b   Evidence to support our hypothesis **is provided by** the results of the experiment.

The results of the experiment .... evidence to support our hypothesis.

c   Your idea **is contradicted by** the evidence.

The evidence .... your idea.

d   Stars **are formed from** clouds of dust and gas.

Clouds of dust and gas .... stars.

e   The experiment **was observed by** the teacher.

The teacher .... the experiment.

Exercise 2 Solar System vocabulary

This exercise gives you more practice in using words that help to describe how the Solar System was formed.

Draw **one** line to match a description to the correct word.

Description		Word
a way of representing an object or process		orbit
a circular path		nebula
a flat surface (that can be imaginary)		model
a cloud of dust and gas in space		axis
turn round and round in the same place		spin
a real or imaginary line that something spins around		plane

> 3.3 Movement in space

Exercise 1 Comparatives and superlatives

In this exercise, will you practise using words that describe differences between things.

Look at **Comparative and superlative adjectives** in the *English Language Skills and Support* section for information about comparatives and superlatives – talking about differences and extremes.

Use some of these words to complete the sentences:

large	larger	the largest
small	smaller	the smallest
fast	faster	the fastest
strong	stronger	the strongest

a   Jupiter has .... mass of all the planets in our Solar System.

b   The strength of gravity on Mars is .... than that on Earth.

c   The speed at which Mercury orbits the Sun is .... than the speed at which the Earth orbits the Sun.

d   The pull of the sun on the planets gets .... as you travel towards the outer edge of the Solar System.

e   The Sun has .... gravity in the Solar System.

f   Neptune has .... speed of orbit of all the planets.

Exercise 2 Getting the words in the right order

Sort out the words in each of these sentences about movement in space.

Remember to use a capital letter (A) and a full stop (.).

You may be able to find more than one way of writing the first two mixed-up sentences.

a   air there space no resistance in is

First way ....

Second way ....

b   place particles it a vacuum is a in with no

First way ....

Second way ....

c   circular planets the the almost orbits of are

....

d orbit gravity planets the the in around Sun keeps

....

e resistance air direction object's in acts the opposite to an movement

....

> 3.4 Tides

Exercise 1 Answering questions

In a test, you often don't need to write a complete sentence in your answer. You can save time by just writing the words that you need.

Each of these answers to a question about tides is correct but they all use more words than are needed. The learner has written full sentences.

Rewrite the answer, making it as short as you can without losing any information. Your answer does **not** need to be a full sentence.

The first one has been done for you.

a Question: What causes the tides?

Long answer: The tides are caused by gravity from the Sun and Moon acting on Earth.

Short answer: gravity from the Sun and Moon acting on Earth

b Question: Explain what is meant by tidal range.

Tidal range means the difference in water depth between high and low tides.

....

....

c What is the approximate time difference between a high tide and a low tide?

The approximate time difference between a high tide and a low tide is 12 hours.

....

....

d Explain why some harbours cannot be used at low tide.

Some harbours cannot be used at low tide because there is no water in them.

....

....

e Why does the Moon have a greater effect on tides than the sun?

The Moon has a greater effect on tides than the Sun because the force of gravity from the Moon is stronger on Earth.

....

....

Exercise 2 Vocabulary practice

This exercise gives you practice in using some words that you have met as you learnt about tides.

Choose suitable words to complete these sentences. Some of the letters in each word have been provided to help you.

The pull of gravity from the _ o_ _ and the Sun on Earth causes a t_d_l force. Tides are most noticeable in _ _ a_ _ _l areas, because we can easily see how the sea level changes along the shore.

Tidal forces affect the l_n_ as well as the sea. The land rises and _a_ _s just a tiny amount each day. These changes in the height of the land are called earth tides.

Earth tides may affect the _r_ _ti_ _ of _ _ l_ _ _ o_ s. They may also affect _ _ _ th_ _a_ _ _ .

> 3.5 Energy

Exercise 1 Describing stores of energy

This exercise gives you more practice in using words that describe stores of energy.

Add a number to the store of energy boxes that match the correct number next to the descriptions.

Description	Store of energy
1 energy stored in a compressed spring	kinetic
2 energy of movement	chemical
3 energy stored in substances such as carbohydrates or fuels	elastic
4 energy transferred by something that is vibrating	light
5 energy from luminous objects	gravitational potential
6 energy stored in hot things, or moving from a hot thing to a colder one	sound
7 energy stored in an object because it is high up	electrical
8 energy transferred as current flows in a circuit	thermal

Exercise 2 Using the correct units

In science, we use units to measure different quantities. This exercise gives you practice in using the correct units and their abbreviations.

Choose the correct unit from the list below for measuring each of the quantities described to complete each sentence. Make sure that you spell the word correctly.

Then choose the correct abbreviation for the unit you have chosen.

Units:	kilograms		joules		newtons	
Abbreviations:	KG	kg	j	J	N	n

a   Weight is measured in .... For example, a book

weighs 1 ....

b   Energy is measured in .... For example, you use about

200 .... of energy to run 100 m.

c   Mass is measured in .... For example, a small elephant has

a mass of 2000 ....

> 3.6 Changes in energy

Exercise 1 Modal verbs

In this exercise, you choose the best modal verb to write sentences about changes in energy.

Look at **Modal verbs** in the *English Language Skills and Support* section for information about modal verbs.

This exercise gives you more practice in describing stores of energy.

Use the words **can** or **must** to complete these sentences.

a   Water .... be heated by burning fuel or using heat from the Sun.

b   Energy changes .... sometimes be dangerous.

c   We .... use diagrams to represent changes in energy.

d   A car .... use fuel to make it move.

e   To make something happen, energy .... be transferred
    or changed.

Exercise 2 Describing energy changes

> In this exercise, you will practise using words to describe what is shown
> in a diagram.

Each of the diagrams shows an energy change.

First, write a sentence to describe what is shown in the diagram. Make sure that you
spell each word correctly.

Then suggest a process or event that could involve this energy change.

The first one has been done for you.

a
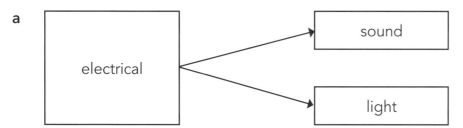

What happens: Electrical energy changes to sound energy and light energy.

Process or event: This happens when a television is switched on.

b

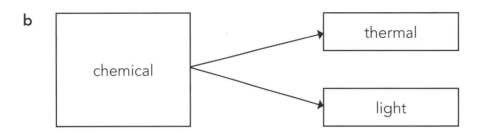

What happens: ....

Process or event: ....

c

```
      ┌─────────┐           ┌─────────┐
      │         │──────────▶│  sound  │
      │ kinetic │           └─────────┘
      │         │           ┌─────────┐
      │         │──────────▶│ thermal │
      └─────────┘           └─────────┘
```

What happens: ....

Process or event: ....

d

```
┌──────────────┐      ┌─────────┐      ┌─────────┐
│ gravitational│─────▶│ kinetic │─────▶│  sound  │
│  potential   │      └─────────┘      └─────────┘
└──────────────┘
```

What happens: ....

Process or event: ....

> 3.7 Where does energy go?

Exercise 1 Writing sentences about energy dissipation

When energy spreads out into the environment so that we cannot use it, we say that it dissipates. In this exercise, you will write sentences about the dissipation of energy.

a   Match the two halves of each sentence so that they make a correct statement about energy.

First half of the sentence	Second half of the sentence
If 40% of the electrical energy supplied to the light bulb changes to light energy,	75% is wasted.
If energy is transferred,	60% is dissipated as heat.
If energy is lost as heat to the environment,	it cannot be recovered.
If only 25% of the energy is changed in a useful way,	some energy is always wasted as heat.

b   Write a sentence of your own about energy being dissipated.

....

....

....

4 > Grouping and identifying organisms

> 4.1 Characteristics of living organisms

Exercise 1 Vocabulary practice

This exercise helps you to remember the seven characteristics of living organisms. You will also practise spelling them correctly.

The letters in the words in the table are jumbled up. Sort out each word and write it in the table.

Then use your correctly spelt words to complete the sentences.

Jumbled words	Correctly spelt words
nioerprudoct	
onratesrpi	
evtnemom	
nointturi	
wghtro	
vitssyenit	
txecoiren	

All types of organism are able to produce new organisms like themselves,

which is called ....

All organisms need to take in nutrients, in a process called ....

Some of these nutrients are used to make new cells, for ....

Some nutrients are broken down inside cells in a process called .... ,
to provide energy for the organisms to use. Some of this energy is used for

....

Organisms are able to detect changes in their environment – a characteristic called

.... Lastly, all organisms need to get rid of toxic and unwanted

substances, which is called ....

> 4.2 Viruses

Exercise 1 Verbs with 'out'

In this exercise, you will practise using verbs such as 'carry out' and 'find out'.

Choose from these words to complete the sentences about viruses. In some of the
sentences, more than one of the verbs can fit – just choose the one that you think
makes the best sense.

carry out   **find out**   **run out**   **work out**

a   Viruses cannot .... any of the characteristics of living things.

b   I cannot finish making my model of a virus because I have ....
    of modelling dough.

c   Scientists use electron microscopes to .... about very small things.

d   He used the evidence to .... that viruses contain protein.

e   If we .... of vaccines, then more people will get influenza.

f   This scientist was the first to .... that influenza viruses
    contain RNA.

g   I am going to use the internet to .... which kind of virus causes colds.

> 4.3 What is a species?

Exercise 1 Vocabulary practice

> This exercise will help you to check that you can use the correct terms to write about species.

Complete the following sentences about species. The first letter of each word has been provided for you.

All jaguars belong to the same s.................... but they are not i....................

to one another. There is v.................... between individual jaguars. Scientists

have measured different s.................... of jaguar and have found that they vary

in size, colour and the pattern of their spots.

In a zoo, a jaguar will sometimes mate with a leopard. Their o.................... are

i.................... In order to produce fertile offspring, an animal must breed with

another member of its own s.................... .

Exercise 2 Using comparatives and superlatives

> When we describe differences between species, or variation within a species, we often use comparatives and superlatives. This exercise gives you practice in describing differences between leaves.

Look at **Comparative and superlative adjectives** in the *English Language Skills and Support* section for information about comparatives and superlatives.

Look at the pictures of the leaves

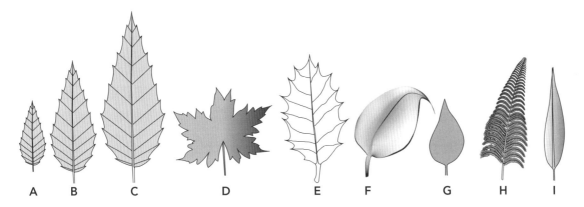

Use the pictures to complete the sentences.

Choose from these words:

longest   longer   narrowest   narrower   most   more

shiniest   shortest   shorter   wider   widest

a   Leaf C is the .... leaf.

b   Leaf B is .... and .... than leaf A.

c   Leaf E is .... prickly than the other leaves.

d   All of the leaves are .... than leaf I.

e   The .... leaf is leaf F.

f   Leaf D is the .... leaf.

> 4.4 Using keys

Exercise 1 Using modal verbs

This exercise will help you think about how to use keys, and gives you practice using modal verbs.

Look at **Modal verbs** in the *English Language Skills and Support* section for information about modal verbs.

Choose the best of these words to complete each of these sentences about using keys. Note that in some cases, more than one answer is possible.

can   cannot   should   should not

a You .... work through each question in turn when you are using a key.

b When you use a key to identify an organism, you .... try to identify more than one organism at the same time.

c A dichotomous key .... have more than two choices each time.

d A key .... have too many different questions.

e A good dichotomous key .... help you to identify an organism quickly.

> 4.5 Constructing keys

Exercise 1 Writing questions to use in a key

A good key has clear, simple questions to answer. In this exercise, you practise selecting a feature that makes one leaf different from the others, and then writing a simple question about that feature.

Look at the pictures of leaves.

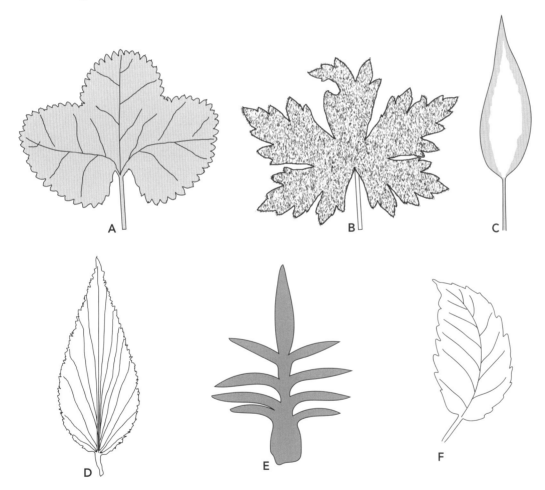

Write a question that could help to separate each leaf from the others, as part of a key. The first one has been done for you.

You may find these words helpful, but you don't have to use them if you don't want to.

curved   jagged   straight   veins

a A question that could help to separate leaf **A** from the other leaves.

Does the leaf have three lobes?

b A question that could help to separate leaf **B** from the other leaves.

....

c A question that could help to separate leaf **C** from the other leaves.

....

d A question that could help to separate leaf **D** from the other leaves.

....

e A question that could help to separate leaf **E** from the other leaves.

....

f A question that could help to separate leaf **F** from the other leaves.

....

5 Properties of materials

> 5.1 Metals and non-metals

Exercise 1 Describing properties

This exercise will help you to check whether you can use the correct words to describe the properties of metals.

Here is a list of some properties of materials.

brittle	conducting	ductile	hard	insulating
malleable	magnetic	shiny	sonorous	strong

Complete the table by writing the property that matches each description. You should use each property once. Make sure that you spell each property correctly.

Description	Property
Many metals reflect light when they are polished.	
Some metals can withstand a large force without breaking.	
Metals can be pulled out into a long wire.	
Some non-metals shatter if you drop them onto a hard surface.	

Description	Property
Many metals make a ringing sound when you hit them.	
Metals can be hammered into different shapes.	
Metals allow electricity to flow through them.	
Pieces of iron can form north and south poles that attract one another.	
Most non-metals do not allow electricity to flow.	
It is difficult to scratch or dent the surface of a metal.	

> 5.2 Comparing metals and non-metals

Exercise 1 Vocabulary practice

In this exercise, you will practise using some of the new words you have learnt in the first two topics in this unit.

Complete these sentences. Use some of these words. You can use each word or phrase once, more than once or not at all.

compare   conduct   contact   crocodile clips   distinguish

lamp   metal   non-metal   produce   property

Zara wants to find an easy way to ………………………… between metals and

non-metals. She decides to find out if they can ………………………… electricity.

She builds this circuit.

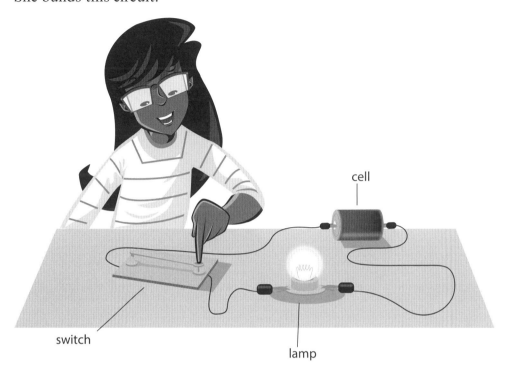

Zara puts the first material to test in the circuit and attaches the ………………………… .

If the lamp does not light, she checks that there is a good ………………………… between

the material and the ………………………… . If the lamp still does not light, she decides

that the material is a ………………………… .

Exercise 2 Connecting words

In this exercise, you have to think carefully about properties of metals and non-metals, and then invent some sentences about them using connecting words.

Write sentences about metals and non-metals, using the connecting words *and*, *but* and *because*. You have a free choice of which metals and which properties to write about.

For example:

Glass is brittle **but** metals are not.

Iron is hard **and** strong.

We use copper to make electrical wires **because** it is ductile **and** a conductor.

a .... and ....

b .... but ....

c .... because ....

d .... and ....

but ....

e .... because ....

and ....

f .... because ....

but ....

g   Now write a sentence about metals and non-metals that uses all three
    connecting words.

....

....

....

> 5.3 Metal mixtures

Exercise 1 Answering questions that have question words

This exercise gives you practice in writing the correct kind of answer to questions that start with different question words.

Look at **Question words** and **Command words** in the *English Language Skills and Support* section for information about question and command words.

Here are some questions and answers about metal mixtures. The questions use the question words *what*, *why*, *which* and *how*.

Draw a line from each question to the correct answer.

Question	Answer
What are aluminium alloys used for?	They are stronger.
Which metals are used to make an aluminium alloy?	For making aeroplanes.
How are aluminium alloys better than pure aluminium?	They are light and strong.
Why are aluminium alloys used for making aeroplanes?	Aluminium, magnesium and copper.

Exercise 2 Answering questions that have command words

This exercise gives you practice in writing the correct kind of answer to questions that have different command words

Look at **Question words** and **Command words** in the *English Language Skills and Support* section for information about question and command words.

For each question:

• <u>underline</u> the command word

• tick (✓) the answer that best answers the question.

a Name the elements that are used to make steel.

Answer 1 carbon and iron ☐

Answer 2 it is an alloy ☐

b Explain why alloys have properties that are different from the metals used to make them.

Answer 1 Alloys are usually harder and stronger than pure metals, which makes them much more useful to us. ☐

Answer 2 Their particles are different sizes, so they are not arranged in regular rows. So the particles can't slide over each other as easily as in a pure metal, which makes the alloy stronger. ☐

c Give one use of bronze.

Answer 1 Bronze is made from copper and tin. It is much harder than copper or tin. It is used for making statues because it looks attractive. ☐

Answer 2 Making statues ☐

d Two metals are mixed together to make an alloy. Describe how this affects the arrangement of particles in the metals.

Answer 1 The regular arrangement of particles is disrupted, so they are not in neat rows. ☐

Answer 2 The alloy is stronger because its particles are rearranged. ☐

> 5.4 Using the properties of materials to separate mixtures

Exercise 1 Naming and using scientific apparatus

> This exercise helps you to check that you know the correct names for different pieces of scientific apparatus.

Look at the pictures of apparatus.

Draw **one** line from the apparatus to its name. Then draw a second line from the apparatus to its use.

Name	Diagram of apparatus	Use
filter funnel		separating an insoluble solid from a liquid
filter paper		cooling a gas to change it to a liquid
condenser		holding a liquid
conical flask		holding a liquid and supporting a funnel
beaker		holding a solution so that it can be heated to remove water
evaporating dish		holding filter paper so that a liquid can be poured into it

> 5.5 Acids and alkalis

Exercise 1 Using modal verbs

This exercise will help you think about keeping safe when using acids and alkalis, and also gives you practice using modal verbs.

Look at **Modal verbs** in the *English Language Skills and Support* section for information modal verbs.

a   Complete these sentences by using each of these words once:

can   should   must

We .... be careful when using acids, because acids

.... be dangerous. If you get acid on your skin, you

.... rinse your skin with lots of water.

b   Complete these sentences, using some of these words. You can use each word once, more than once or not at all.

can   must   if   will

You .... find alkalis in many cleaning products. ....

a strong alkali gets onto your skin, it .... harm it. Alkalis

.... be diluted with water. This makes them less harmful.

Exercise 2 Vocabulary practice

This exercise will let you check that you know the meanings of the new words you have used in this topic.

Write the word that matches each of these descriptions. Choose from these words:

acid	alkali	corrosive	flammable
harmful	irritate	oxidising	toxic

a   Examples include hydrochloric and citric. ....

b   Can damage substances that it comes into contact with by a chemical reaction.

   ....

c   Make your eyes or skin itch and sting. ....

d   Burns easily. ....

e   Examples include sodium hydroxide and some cleaning fluids. ....

f   Poisonous. ....

g   Can cause some kind of damage. ....

h   Has this hazard symbol: ....

› 5.6 Indicators and the pH scale

Exercise 1 Comparatives

This exercise gives you practice in using comparatives, and also checks that you understand the pH scale.

Look at **Comparative and superlative adjectives** in the *English Language Skills and Support* section for information about comparatives and superlatives.

For each sentence, make a comparative from the word in **bold** to complete the sentence.

a   low

This liquid is neutral, so its pH is .... than that of the alkali.

b   acidic

An indicator can show whether one substance is .... than another.

c   alkaline

The universal indicator went purple in this liquid and red in the other one, so

this one is ....

d   low

The litmus paper turned red in the lemon juice but not in the water, so

the lemon juice has a .... pH than the water.

e   high

Alkalis are .... on the pH scale than acids.

Exercise 2 Recording observations and conclusions in a table

In this exercise, you will check that you understand the words describing parts of a results table, and that you can construct and complete one successfully.

Look at **Results tables** in the *English Language Skills and Support* section for information about results tables.

Marcus adds universal indicator to some different liquids.

These are his observations.

lemon juice, orange
tap water, green
vinegar, red
cleaning fluid, purple
fizzy drink, orange-red
sea water, blue-green

a   Draw a table with three columns and seven rows.

b   Write the heading **Substance** at the top of the first column.

c   Write the heading **Colour with universal indicator** at the top of the second column.

d   Write the heading **pH** at the top of the last column.

e   Fill in Marcus's observations.

f   Use your knowledge of universal indicator (or look it up in Topic 5.6 in the Learner's Book) to work out the pH of each liquid, then write this pH in the last column.

6 > Earth physics

> 6.1 Sound waves

Exercise 1 Observations and conclusions

It is easy to mix up an observation and a conclusion. In this exercise, you will practise using the words observation and conclusion correctly.

Look at **Results tables** in the *English Language Skills and Support* section for information about observation and conclusions.

An **observation** is something that you see, hear, smell, or sense in some other way. A **conclusion** is something you can work out from your observations or other results.

Here is an example.

Marcus puts his ear on the desk while Zara taps on the desk. This makes the wood vibrate. Marcus can hear the sound of Zara tapping. This shows that sound can travel through wood.

What **observation** does Marcus make? He can hear the sound of Zara tapping

....

....

What is the **conclusion** that Marcus makes? Sound can travel through wood ....

....

....

a   Arun puts a glass jar over an electric bell. He closes the switch in the circuit and hears the bell ringing. He switches on a pump that removes all the air from the jar. Now he cannot hear the bell. He decides that this means that sound cannot travel through a vacuum.

bell jar

to pump

What **observation** does Arun make? ....

....

What is the **conclusion** that Arun makes? ....

....

b   Marcus and Arun each hold a paper cup. The cups are joined by a long string.

Marcus holds one cup against his ear, while Arun speaks into the other cup. When the string is held taut, Marcus can hear Arun, but he cannot hear him if the string is slack.

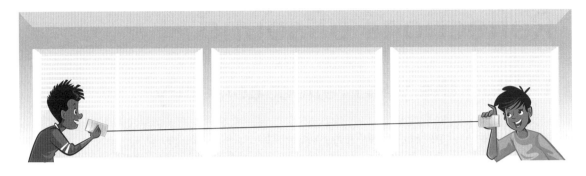

The boys think this is because sound waves move more easily through the taut string than the slack string.

What **observation** do the boys make? ....……..........

....

What is the **conclusion** that the boys make? ....

....

Exercise 2 Vocabulary practice

Here is a quick check on whether you remember the meanings of some of the new words you have used in this topic.

Draw a line to connect each word to its meaning.

Word	Meaning
vibrating	moving backwards and forwards quickly, over and over again
loudness	how high or low a sound is on a musical scale
pitch	something that contains particles that sound can travel through
medium	it is about 1200 km per hour
speed of sound	how noisy a sound is

> 6.2 Reflections of sound

Exercise 1 Using the verb reflect correctly

You can use the verb reflect in the active or passive form.

If you use these forms incorrectly, you make statements that are not scientifically correct.

Active:

The mirror reflects light from the torch. ✓

The torch reflects light onto the mirror. ✗

Passive:

The light is reflected by the mirror. ✓

Light is reflected on the mirror by the torch. ✗

a   Sofia plays her trumpet. She hears an echo of the sound that the trumpet makes. Tick (✓) each sentence that correctly describes what happens.

Put a cross next to each sentence that is wrong.

The sound of the trumpet reflects off the wall.   ☐

The wall reflects the sound of the trumpet.   ☐

The trumpet reflects its sound onto the wall.   ☐

The sound of the trumpet is reflected by the wall.   ☐

The sound reflects onto the wall.   ☐

b (Circle) the word that correctly completes each sentence.

You hear an echo because sound is reflected **by** / **to** a surface.

When the bell rings, the window reflects sound **onto** / **from** the bell.

Bats find their food by detecting sound waves reflected **from** / **onto** insects.

> 6.3 Structure of the Earth

Exercise 1 Correcting statements about the structure of the Earth

In this exercise, you will practise reading a sentence carefully, and also writing your own sentences, using correct English and spelling.

Decide whether each of the following statements is correct. Put a tick (✓) or cross (✗) next to each one.

If the statement is **not** correct, write a correct statement underneath. Write a complete sentence and make sure to get the spelling right.

a The mantle is the deepest layer in the Earth. ☐

....

....

b The outer part of the Earth's core contains molten iron but the inner core is solid. ☐

....

....

c The Earth's crust is made up of several tectonic plates that can move around. ☐

....

....

d Continental drift is caused when strong water currents cause the
continents to move. □

....

....

e Magma is found under the oceans but not under the continents. □

....

....

> 6.4 Changes in the Earth

Exercise 1 Spelling practice

There are a lot of new words in this topic. Can you spell them all correctly?

There are **ten** spelling mistakes in these sentences. Circle each word that is spelt
incorrectly. Then write the correct spelling in the space at the end.

The Earth's crust is made of many teptonic plates, which meet at
plate boundaries. Where one plate dives underneath another, there
is a subdiction zone. The great forces produced here can cause
earthquakes. If the earthquaike has a large magnitued, it can cause a
lot of damage to cities and roads.

Cracks or fractures in the Earth's crust can also form at plate
boundaries, allowing magna to rise up and form volcanoes. Once it is on
the surface, this liquid rock is called larva. Some volcanoes that were
active in the past are now 'sleeping' or dorment. Other volcanoes will
never errupt again, and they are said to be extingct.

When two tectonic plates push against each other, they can make the
Earth's crust crumple up. This forms fould mountains.

....

....

....

....

....

> 6.5 Solar and lunar eclipses

Exercise 1 Using adjectives

In this exercise, you will practise using some of the new adjectives that you have learnt in this topic.

Choose the best adjective to complete each of these sentences. Circle your choice.

a   Light cannot pass through **a transparent** / **an opaque** object.

b   A shadow is formed when light rays are blocked by **a transparent** / **an opaque** object.

c   An eclipse that is caused when the Moon comes between the Sun and the Earth is called a **solar** / **lunar** eclipse.

d   An eclipse that is caused when the Earth comes between the Sun and the Moon is called a **solar** / **lunar** eclipse.

e   If the Moon does not cover all of the Sun, we see a **partial** / **total** eclipse.

7 ▶ Microorganisms in the environment

› 7.1 Microorganisms

Exercise 1 Unusual singular and plural words

> Several of the words in this topic have unusual plurals. In this exercise, you will practise using these words correctly.

Circle the word that better completes each of these sentences.

a   Bacteria **is** / **are** a type of single-celled microorganism.

b   Mushrooms, toadstools and yeast are **fungi** / **fungus**.

c   If you look at pond water through a microscope, you may be able to see **protozoa** / **protozoas** and **alga** / **algae**.

d   A virus is smaller than a **bacteria** / **bacterium**.

e   This **protozoan** / **protozoa** has a cell like an animal cell.

f   A **fungu** / **fungus** spends most of its life as microscopic threads underground.

Exercise 2 Vocabulary practice

> This exercise checks that you understand four important terms used
> in this topic.

Label the diagram with the following words.

Use each word in the list once only.

Petri dish   **sterile agar jelly**   **colony of bacteria**   **colony of fungi**

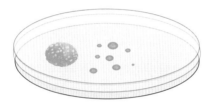

› 7.2 Food chains and webs

Exercise 1 Active and passive verbs

> You can use the verbs eat and are eaten by to describe food chains.
> This exercise gives you practice in using both of these.

Look at **Active and passive verbs** in the *English Language Skills and Support* section for information about active and passive verbs.

a   Here is a food chain.

water plant → tadpole → grass snake → egret

Tadpoles eat water plants.

Water plants are eaten by tadpoles.

Complete each of these sentences. Use the words **eat** or **are eaten by**.

Grass snakes ………………………………… tadpoles.

Egrets ………………………………… grass snakes.

Tadpoles ………………………………… grass snakes.

Grass snakes ………………………………… egrets.

b These sentences describe a food chain. Draw the food chain.
Springbok eat grass.
Springbok are eaten by lions.

c The diagram shows a food web.

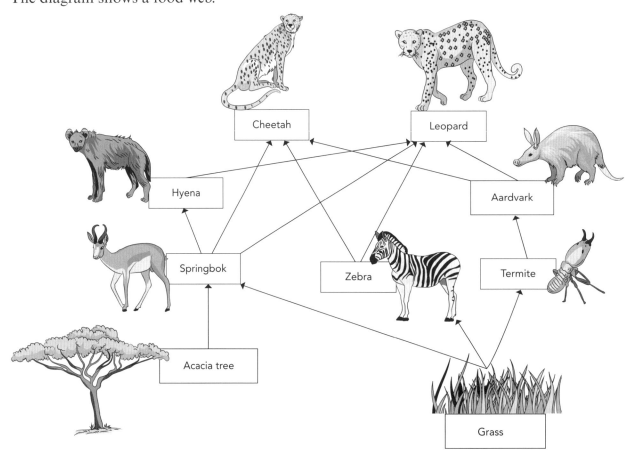

Cheetahs eat zebras.

Write **three** more sentences describing part of the food web, using the word **eat**.

....

....

....

d Termites are eaten by aardvarks.

Write **three** more sentences describing part of the food web, using the words **are eaten by**.

....

....

....

Exercise 2 Food web vocabulary

There is a lot of special vocabulary to use when you read or write about food webs. This exercise will help you to make sure that you understand all of these terms.

Use words from the list to complete the sentences.

You must use each word once.

food chains   food web   producer   consumer   herbivores

carnivores   predators   prey   energy transfer

a A .... is an organism that makes food, using energy from sunlight.

b A .... is an organism that gets its energy by eating producers or other consumers.

c Animals that eat only plants are called ....

d Animals that eat other animals are called ....

e Lions kill and eat zebras. Lions are .... and zebras are

the lions' ....

f The arrows in a food chain show the direction of ....
from one organism to the next.

g A diagram showing many interconnecting .... is called

a ....

› 7.3 Microorganisms and decay

Exercise 1 Comparatives and superlatives

This exercise asks you to use comparatives and superlatives to describe the
results of an experiment about microorganisms and decay.

Look at **Comparative and superlative adjectives** in the *English Language
Skills and Support* section for information about using comparatives and
superlatives.

Arun put three pieces of bread onto three paper plates. He put water onto two
of them.

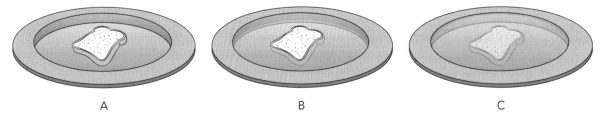

A   B   C

Arun covered all the pieces of bread. He left the pieces of bread in a warm place.

The diagram shows the pieces of bread after five days.

A   B   C

Complete the sentences, using some of these words. You may use each word once, more than once or not at all.

more	most	least
dry	drier	driest
mouldy	mouldier	mouldiest

a   Arun put .... water onto piece C than onto piece B.

b   Piece A was the .... piece of bread of the three.

c   At the end of the experiment, piece B was .... than piece A.

d   The .... piece of bread was piece C.

Exercise 2 Writing sentences about microorganisms and decay

Writing your own sentences is a good way to practise thinking about the facts that you have learnt in this topic.

Use these starters to write your own sentences. Try to give correct and useful information, and to spell each word correctly.

Here is an example.

Decomposers are organisms that break down organic material such as dead plants.

a   The words **decay** and **rot** both mean ....

....

b   A **mouldy** apple..

....

c   **Organic matter** is ....

....

> 7.4 Microorganisms in food webs

Exercise 1 Using 'if' and 'will' to make predictions

This exercise gives you practice in using correct English to make predictions about food webs.

Look at **Making predictions** in the *English Language Skills and Support* section for information about making predictions.

The diagram shows a food web that includes microorganisms.

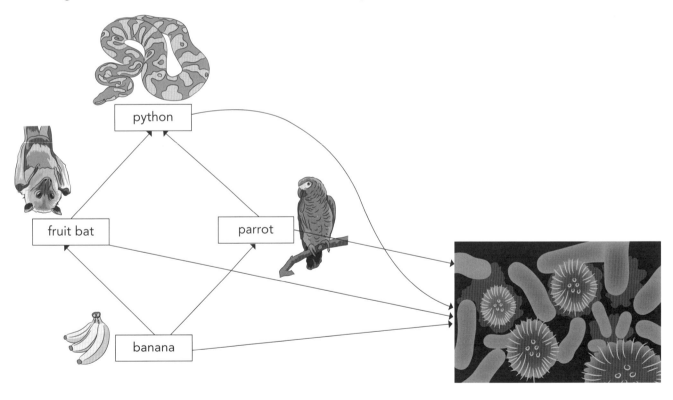

a   Here is a prediction about what might happen if something changes in the food web.

If all the parrots are killed, there will be more bananas so the fruit bats will have more food.

Make four predictions of your own about the food web, using the words *if* and *will*.

Prediction 1: ....

....

Prediction 2: ....

....

Prediction 3: ....

....

Prediction 4: ....

....

b   Use these sentence starters to make predictions. Use the word in **bold** as part of your prediction.

dung

If there are no decomposers, ...

....

nutrient

If dead organisms do not decay, ...

....

8 > Changes to materials

> 8.1 Simple chemical reactions

Exercise 1 Positive and negative statements

> This exercise checks that you understand what happens during a chemical reaction, and that you can use the new words in this topic correctly. You will also try writing some sentences yourself, to test a friend.

Draw a (circle) around the correct words to complete each sentence.

a   In a chemical reaction, new substances **are** / **are not** formed.

b   When you mix iron and sulfur together without heating them, iron sulfide **is** / **is not** produced.

c   Burning **is** / **is not** a chemical reaction.

d   Reactants **are** / **are not** formed by a chemical reaction.

e   In a mixture of iron and sulfur, the two elements **are** / **are not** combined.

f   The new substances that are formed after a chemical reaction has happened **are** / **are not** called products.

Now write two sentences like this of your own, to try out on a friend.

g   Use the words **reacted** and **water** in your sentences.

First sentence: ....

....

Second sentence: ....

....

Exercise 2 Observations and conclusions

When you do experiments, you make observations about what happens. You can use the observations to make conclusions. In this exercise, you must decide whether a statement is describing an observation or a conclusion.

Look at **Results tables** in the *English Language Skills and Support* section for information about observations and conclusions.

These four groups of statements describe four processes or reactions.

For each statement, write **O** if it is an observation and **C** if is a conclusion.

When magnesium is burnt in oxygen, a white powder is formed. ....

The white powder is a new substance, and it cannot be changed back to magnesium

and oxygen. ....

A chemical change has taken place. ....

When liquid water is cooled below 0 °C, it changes to ice. ....

If you heat the ice, it changes back to liquid water. ....

Changing from liquid to ice is a physical change. ....

When potassium is put into water, bubbles are produced. ....

When I put a lighted splint into the tube, there is a squeaky pop. ....

The gas is hydrogen. ....

When iron and sulfur are heated together, a new substance is formed. ....

Now you cannot separate the iron from the sulfur. ....

A chemical change has taken place. ....

› 8.2 Neutralisation

Exercise 1 Verbs, nouns and adjectives

In this exercise, you will practise making nouns from verbs, and then choose a verb, noun or adjective to complete some sentences.

a You can often make a noun from a verb by adding -*ion* to it. Sometimes you need to add some other letters before the -*ion*.

Write a noun that matches each of these verbs. The first one has been done for you.

Verb	Noun
react	reaction
neutralise	
filter	
digest	

b Circle the correct words to complete each sentence.

a **Acids** / **Acidic** have a low pH. If a solution has pH lower than 7, it is **acids**. / **acidic**.

b Marcus **filters** / **filter** / **filtrate** the mixture of soil and water by pouring it through some **filters** / **filter** / **filtrate** paper. The liquid that runs through the paper is the **filters**. / **filter**. / **filtrate**.

c **Neutralisation** / **Neutralise** / **Neutral** happens when an acid and alkali are mixed together. If you use a burette to add the correct quantity of acid to an alkali, you can make a **neutralisation** / **neutralise** / **neutral** solution.

Exercise 2 Naming and using scientific apparatus

In this exercise, you will make sure that you can use the correct names for some pieces of scientific apparatus.

Here are some pictures of apparatus that you can use when you are doing neutralisation experiments.

Draw lines from each piece of apparatus to its name and its use.

Name	Diagram of apparatus	Use
conical flask		carefully adding measured volumes of a liquid
burette		container for a liquid that can also support a filter funnel
filter funnel		supporting filter paper so a liquid can be poured through it
safety glasses		protecting your eyes from splashes
beaker		container for a liquid

> 8.3 Investigating acids and alkalis

Exercise 1 Language for planning experiments

When we plan experiments, we need to think about the different kinds of variables. In this exercise, you will practise using these words correctly.

Look at **Language for planning experiments** in the *English Language Skills and Support* section for information about language to use for planning experiments.

Use these words and phrases to complete the sentences. You can use each word or phrase once, more than once or not at all.

dependent variable   fair test   independent variable

a   A variable is something that can change. When you do a

.... experiment, you must only change the

....

b   Sofia investigates remedies for indigestion. She wants to find out which indigestion

powder is best at neutralising an acid.

Her .... is the kind of indigestion powder that

she uses. The .... is the number of spatulas of

powder that she has to add to the acid to neutralise it.

> 8.4 Detecting chemical reactions

Exercise 1 Naming chemicals

This exercise gives you practice in using the correct names for several different chemical substances.

Choose words from the list to write the two-word name of each chemical that is described.

You should use each word once, except for one word that you will use twice.

Make sure that you write the words in the correct order.

acid	carbon	copper	dioxide	hydrochloric
hydrogen	hydroxide	indicator	oxide	nitrate
peroxide	silver	sodium	sulfate	universal

a   A liquid with a low pH that reacts with metals to produce hydrogen.

....

b   A black powder that reacts with sulfuric acid. It is a compound of copper and oxygen.

....

c   A gas containing carbon and oxygen, which makes limewater go cloudy.

....

d   A blue substance that dissolves to make a bright blue solution.

....

e   A solution that you can use to find the pH of a liquid.

....

f   An alkali.

....

g A liquid that looks like water, but that gives off a gas that will relight a glowing splint when you add manganese dioxide to it.

....

h When you mix this chemical with calcium chloride, a precipitate of silver chloride is formed.

....

9 ▶ Electricity

❯ 9.1 Flow of electricity

Exercise 1 Active and passive verbs

This exercise gives you practice in using words about electrical circuits, and also in using active verbs. Using an active verb, rather than a passive verb, to write a sentence is often a simpler way of describing things.

Look at **Active and passive verbs** in the *English Language Skills and Support* section for information about active and passive verbs.

Each of these sentences contains a passive verb.

Rewrite the sentence using an active verb.

The first one has been done for you.

a   Chemical energy **is stored** by a cell.

   A cell stores chemical energy.

b   Electrons **are pushed** around a circuit by a cell.

   ....

c   Negative charges **are repelled** by other negative charges.

   ....

d   Electrons **are attracted** by the positive terminal of a battery.

   ....

e   A current **is produced** when electrons move in a circuit.

   ....

f   Electricity **is conducted** through metals because their electrons are free to move.

....

g   The components in an electrical circuit **can be modelled** by people holding a loop of string.

....

› 9.2 Electrical circuits

Exercise 1 Modal verbs and making predictions

This exercise will help you to think about electrical circuits, and also to use modal verbs.

Look at **Modal verbs** in the *English Language Skills and Support* section for information about modal verbs.

Complete these sentences, choosing words from the list.

can   must   must not   will   will not

a   When you draw a circuit diagram, you .... use the correct circuit symbols.

b   You .... show this circuit by drawing the components, or by using circuit symbols.

c   If there is a gap in the circuit, it .... allow current to flow.

d   You .... use an ammeter to measure the current in a circuit.

e   This circuit .... be used to make a buzzer work.

f   If you do not close the switch in the circuit, the bell .... ring.

g   In a circuit diagram, you .... draw lines going through the components.

h   If the electrons move faster, the current .... increase.

> 9.3 Measuring the flow of current

Exercise 1 Making predictions

In this exercise, you will practise using 'if' and 'will' to make predictions about electrical current.

Complete the sentences by adding words from the list.

become zero   decrease   increase   stay the same

a   If the electrons move faster, the current will ....

b   If you put the ammeter in a different place in the series circuit, the current will ....

c   If there is a gap in the circuit, the current will ....

d   If the electrons move more slowly, the reading on the ammeter will ....

Exercise 2 Vocabulary practice – circuit components

This exercise checks that you know the correct names for four components of electrical circuits, and also their symbols and uses.

Draw lines to connect each circuit component to its name, symbol and use.

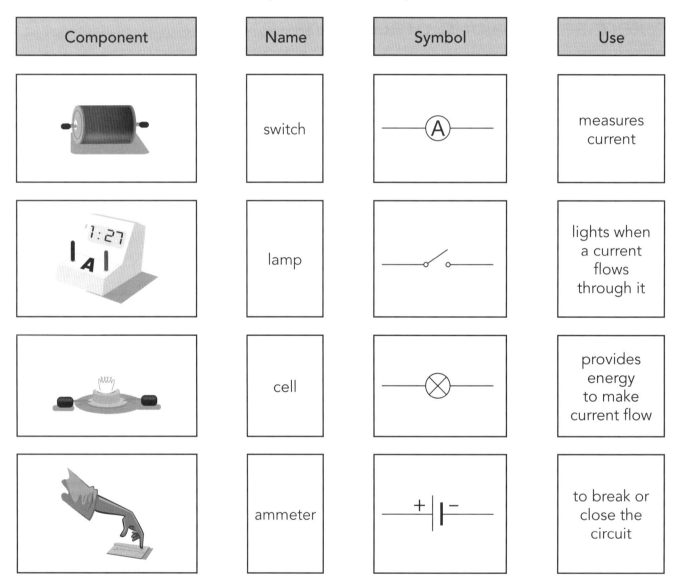

Component	Name	Symbol	Use
	switch	—(A)—	measures current
	lamp	—o o—	lights when a current flows through it
	cell	—⊗—	provides energy to make current flow
	ammeter	—+ ┤├ −—	to break or close the circuit

> 9.4 Conductors and insulators

Exercise 1 Putting words in the correct order

If you use the correct words, but in the wrong order, your sentence does not make sense. In this exercise, you will sort words to make sentences about conductors and insulators.

Look at **Word order** in the *English Language Skills and Support* section for information about putting words in the correct order in a sentence.

Write each sentence with the words in the correct order. Remember to use a capital letter (for example, A) and full stop (.).

Sentences **e** and **f** could be written as questions. You could try writing them first as a statement and then as a question.

a   to flow conductors allow current

    ....

b   current flow not insulators do allow to

    ....

c   move freely electrons can in a conductor

    ....

d   freely in electrons cannot an move insulator

    ....

e   all conductors are metals

    ....

    ....

f   an insulator is plastic

    ....

    ....

> 9.5 Adding or removing components

Exercise 1 The more..., the more...

In this exercise, you will practise using a sentence structure that you will often use in science.

Look at **Comparative and Superlative Adjectives** in the *English Language Skills and Support* section for information about sentence structure.

Complete each of the following sentences.

Use these words:

> **greater**   less   more   smaller

a   The more cells in the circuit, the .... the current.

b   The more lamps in the circuit, the .... the current.

c   The more lamps in the series circuit, the .... bright they look.

d   The more cells in the circuit, the .... electrical energy transferred by the electrons.

e   The more lamps in the circuit, the .... slowly the electrons move.